CW01023899

WE WERE HERE

THE AMBER POETS

Artur Dron'

We Were Here

Translated from the Ukrainian by
Yuliya Musakovska

Edited by Hugh Roberts and Helen Vassallo
with Fiona Benson and Charlotte Shevchenko Knight

The Amber Poets
Series Editor
Michael Tate

JANTAR PUBLISHING
London 2024

THE AMBER POETS
Book 1

We Were Here
Artur Dron'
All rights reserved.

First published in London, Great Britain, in 2024 by
Jantar Publishing Ltd
www.jantarpublishing.com

First published in Ukrainian by Vydavnytstvo Staroho Leva
(The Old Lion Publishing House) in 2023 as
Тут були ми

Original text © Artur Dron' 2023
Foreword © Hugh Roberts 2024

Translation © Yuliya Musakovska 2024
Cover and book design © Davor Pukljak 2024

A CIP record of this book is available from the British Library
ISBN 978-1-914990-26-7

This book has been published with the support of
the Translate Ukraine Translation Program and the University of Exeter.

**UKRAINIAN
//|||BOOK
INSTITUTE**

Contents

II. Voices

III. The Beginning, The End, The Beginning

Foreword

Artur Dron' has always seen literature as integral to his identity. His debut poetry collection, *Dormitory No. 6*, was published by Triada Plus in 2020. When Russia's full-scale war on Ukraine began on 24 February 2022, he was working as an event manager at the Old Lion Publishing House in Lviv. Within weeks, he volunteered for the 125th Separate Territorial Defence Brigade, also from Lviv, and has been serving with them ever since. *We Were Here* is his second book of poetry; it was published by Old Lion to great acclaim in 2023. Dron' was 22 years old at the time.

Why do we need poetry at a time of war? As Artur Dron' concedes in his Afterword, poetry cannot protect anyone physically or bring them back to life, yet he, like so many of his comrades on both the front line and the home front, has turned to poetry amid the horror. The answer the soldier-poet gives to the question of why we need poetry is noteworthy: *to feel less lonely*. The power of words lies in the opportunity they afford to share experience and emotion. They cannot ease the trauma, but they are a reminder that no-one faces it alone. For the most important thing is not that brutal force has come to Ukraine, but that Ukrainians have joined forces in a myriad of ways to hold the line: this is part of what *we were here* means.

We Were Here echoes the famous words of Volodymyr Zelensky in his selfie video, flanked by the prime minister and other officials, from Kyiv on the night of 25 February 2022: *we are all here*. That Zelensky kept saying *'Tut'* (here) is no coincidence, for *here* was what was under existential threat and a message was going out to Ukraine and the world: 'Our soldiers are here. The citizens are here, and we are here. We defend our independence, our state, and we will continue to do so.' Whether knowingly or not, those words and all they mean reverberate through Artur Dron's collection, which tells of what has happened to those soldiers and citizens. It also looks forwards because, as he says, 'We are not going anywhere.' The proceeds of Dron's book in Ukrainian, which is illustrated by children's pictures posted to soldiers on the front line, are going to the Voices of Children Charity Foundation. There is no contradiction in looking unflinchingly at what people have been through and all that has been lost and simultaneously drawing on spiritual reserves of strength to pass them onto the future: 'When we speak of hope / we're actually speaking / of children', as he says in his poem, 'Children'. The importance of children is felt throughout the collection for not only do the soldiers fight to offer protection to those unable to defend themselves, but when they take off their helmets and body armour, they become children again themselves.

The poems in *We Were Here* were written on the front line, yet they carry over to those beyond, to those on the home front in Ukraine so the lines blur and intense individual expression conveys wider collective experience which, through translation, extends to those of us who were not there. As Dron' writes in the opening poem:

this bitter Love
which becomes your own,
depends on those
on the line.
And those
behind it.

Love is the alpha and the omega of *We Were Here*. Hence the extraordinary final poem, which reimagines St Paul's First Letter to the Corinthians, chapter 13, arrives back where the collection started:

Because sometimes when the shelling ceases,
friends close love's eyes,
wrap it in sleeping bags
and carry it away.

And then it passes on
to the living.

To translate Artur Dron' is therefore to attempt to stay as true as possible to the spirit of his work, which is a spirit of love in the face of the death and destruction Russia has brought to Ukraine. We are fortunate that Yuliya Musakovska, herself an acclaimed Ukrainian poet and translator, has undertaken this translation into English. Not only has she already compiled and edited Dron's translation into Swedish, but she also knows Dron' personally, so has been able to discuss his poems during his periods of leave and even occasionally via

Messenger. These conversations have been at the forefront of our editorial discussions, allowing a small team of poets, translators and academics to support Musakovska in her tireless efforts to share Ukrainian cultural voices at a time when they are so endangered.

If we choose to be open to them, Artur Dron' offers otherwise unimaginable perspectives to those of us without direct personal experience of war. It gives us insights into, for instance, the resident of Partisan Street who sees off a Russian soldier with her slipper, full of 'Ukrainian woman rage' after they gratuitously run over a playground with their tank. To live on Partisan Street is to live on hope, she says: she stands for so many small but significant acts of resistance in a conflict where being bipartisan feels untenable. It is as if we are being invited to join her neighbourhood and share a personal power and resilience from which those of us living apparently more privileged lives may have a lot to learn.

Yet this can only go so far, as some experiences will remain out of reach. The regiment unofficially adopt Kiryukha, the last child remaining on Partisan Street. No-one will say *we were here* or try to express what it was like to be huddled together in that freezing cold winter in dugouts won back from the Russians, for who could possibly understand? And who other than Kiryukha could ever recall the most important thing, the bag he found from Santa with Snickers bars and tangerines, 'the ones with seeds, but oh so sweet'? Such little, nameless acts of kindness and of love are the stuff of *We Were Here* and its spiritual offering to those of us who were never there.

Among the many tragedies of Russia's war on Ukraine is the killing of well over a hundred writers and artists as recorded by PEN Ukraine, a stark illustration of how endangered Ukrainian voices are. Artur Dron' pays homage to them. In 'Ukrainian Literature', he writes:

> They say literature
> is about words and the silence between them
> ours now
> contains more of the latter

We Were Here remembers and reveres the dead. Witness the power of 'The Izyum Communion', concerning the mass graves uncovered in that city following its liberation, all the bodies being figures of Christ:

> These are our bodies
> broken for us.
> But no forgiveness of sin.

Artur Dron' is part of a centuries-old lineage of Ukrainian writers and poets who have written in defiance of the imperial Russian force that has sought repeatedly to oppress and erase their people, language and identity. In the pages that follow, the prominent poet, translator, and dissident Vasyl Stus, who died in a Soviet labour camp in 1985, appears as a brother-in-arms. The dead are not truly gone, they join forces with the living, as Dron' says in his poem, 'Stus':

Your dead are with you;
they're on your side.
No one turns a blind eye,
no-one's above the fray.
Just fury, fury, fury.
No living man
will be scared
no dead man
killed.

***

Perhaps the spiritual value of human existence only becomes obvious when its vulnerability is most apparent. What is true of individuals is also the case of the communities where they live, from the smallest groups to entire languages, cultures and nation states. Over centuries, countless collectives have been destroyed for the sake of the arrogance and greed of those who wield power against them. A collective that stands for its freedom and independence in the face of seemingly overwhelming force, and that expresses the best of the human spirit in the form of poetry and love, is worthy of anyone's attention. We may not be able to join Artur Dron' in saying that we were here, yet through the message his poetry carries across from the front line we can be in no doubt about where we stand.

Hugh Roberts
Exeter, August 2024

Acknowledgements

We are grateful to the Ukrainian Book Institute for their award of a 2024 Translate Ukraine grant for this book, which has supported all aspects of its publication.

We also benefited from translational funding awarded by the University of Exeter to recognize the vital contribution of the poets Fiona Benson and Charlotte Shevchenko Knight to the editing process.

Yuliya Musakovska first presented us with the poetry of Artur Dron' in July 2023 during an event funded by the Department of Languages, Cultures, and Visual Studies at the University of Exeter, 'Translating Cultures with UNESCO Cities of Literature'. We gratefully acknowledge our friends at Exeter and Lviv Cities of Literature, without whom this encounter would not have happened.

This book is dedicated to my fellow fighters:
the living and the dead.

"Write about what's inside us."
Senior Sergeant Andriy Kamynskyi

***

Before you reach the line,
cherish this Love
that grows like wild brambles.
Devotion of a sergeant,
a child, a dog.
The weeping
I can never weep out.

You reach the line
and stamp your footprints.
You hold the line,
hold all together
and stay in this October forever
as if under order.

Because this Love
which cuts like a dull knife,
this bitter Love
which becomes your own,
depends on those
on the line.
And those
behind it.

I.
The Field of Mars

The Field of Mars is another name for the Lychakiv military cemetery in Lviv, Ukraine, which has added hundreds of new graves since the beginning of the Russian full-scale invasion.

***

Pope John Paul the Second
said in those old carefree times
in Lviv:
"Rain falls, children grow."

Dear Saint John Paul,
I grew up under this rain.
But now, in such a winter,
nothing is free:
snow and soldiers must fall.
Soldiers fall, children grow.
Soldiers fall, children grow.

The Field of Mars

1

A soldier kneels in front of a woman,
just like she used to kneel in front of her son
to tie his laces up
when he was small.

He avoids looking the woman in the eye
just like her son used to do when he was small
and felt ashamed.

The soldier says:
"Here, woman, a flag for you.
Love it."

2

As he was leaving she gave him
a picture she drew as a child –
a coloured flower that took up the whole page
with the crayoned inscription:
"God protekts us."
She drew it fifteen years ago,
she wasn't yet seven.
And neither was he.

Now she thinks:
funny, I wonder
what would have happened
if I'd spelt it correctly?

3

Before her son's return,
she dreamt of storks.
When her grandson went to fight,
the old woman went to bed early
and slept late.

Now she often comes to this field
and stands watching
as if she too will soon fly.

She stands watching
like a big stork
who does not want
to be consoled.

***

A vase with fresh flowers
has fallen over.
Let me put that straight, I say
to a photo on a cross.

I pick up the vase and find
a note.
"Happy anniversary to us, honey bun.
I love you."

Wife

I must have seen,
must have known
it was him.
My sons tried to hold me up
but I told them: "I can stand".

What can I say?
My beloved sleeps.
All blue,
they brought him back so late.

But, you know,
we will see each other again.
We'll celebrate
so many anniversaries together.

God, I'm so looking forward to meeting him again.
I'm so scared of not believing in anything.
God, I'm so looking forward to meeting him again.

Can I pray for you all?

Ivan

I was going to give you a bicycle
as a gift after the war.
Just like you'd described –
with a basket and panniers
to go to the store.

I'm sorry I was the first
to ask what your dreams were.
And no, I don't know
how deep the Dnipro River goes
but isn't it a strange world
we were trying to protect, old man?

Our last day has begun,
but it's just typical:
all the stores are closed.
The last shelling has ended,
but all I can hear
is a bicycle bell.

Romko

Only he ever touched
the grill in the yard.

"Romko, marinate the shashlyk."
"Romko, you start the fire,
and we'll make the salad."
The same thing each time we returned
from combat duty.

But that evening as our platoon commander
cleaned the backpack, he kept saying:
"Romko's blood is all over it. His blood's all over it."

Then we sat at the table,
ate a radish salad
and meat
fried in a pan.

***

I read it on Facebook, I never miss
any posts from your boys.

"Twenty-eight years old,
    died fighting for Ukraine…"

I want to ask after him so badly
but I'm afraid to.
I think about the box
you told me about.
What was it like to pack up his things?
How do you live
with all this?

Tank Crewmen

"Camel! Camel!" – a tank squaddie calls
to his commander.

He passes the tank tread
which is still warm.

"Camel! Camel!" – he calls out
in the way only a living tank crewman
calls to a dead one.

***

The less often
you use the word 'war'
the more they'll trust
your poems.

Tell it the way it was.
He was shot by his own side
by accident, no one wanted this.
Already dark in the winter forest,
Wagner squad advancing,
and the fight so long.
He was crawling out to one of the wounded
and got lost in the twilight;
they didn't recognize him.

Don't write 'war', instead write:
they will all – every last one of them –
always be caught in the web
of that night.

The Wagner Group is a Russian mercenary group that has conducted military
operations around the world on behalf of the Russian government. Wagner
operatives have been accused of war crimes including murder, torture, rape and
robbery of civilians, as well as of torturing and killing those accused of desertion.

Ukrainian Literature

Who never got to be heard
in our poetry world?
Who never made it
in the literary scene?
Whose working title and biography
are now crammed onto a grave marker?

They say literature
is about words and the silence between them.
Ours now
contains more of the latter.

Flower Seller

Chrysanthemums, carnations.
They're the ones that last the longest.
But yeah, you could take
roses, too.
They're more lavish.
Take a look and I'll
find a ribbon.

How many would you like?
Eight?
Ten?

The District

Was there ever a time without such piercing pain?
Tomorrow they'll bring his body back.
His district is waiting for him,
the whole city is waiting.

Our hearts are weighed down, our eyes sad,
but we are singing at death these days:
"O death where is your sting?"

Nothing is new in our district now.
Our hearts are weighed down, our tears are salty.
We go to bed early, but I cannot sleep.

Grass in our district still grows.
Dead soldiers are often brought back to us.
but you can't stop the spring.

Priests and teachers tell us,
we shall gather on another earth
when all things will pass.

These days we sing at death in unison:
"We'll meet again, everyone in our district –
no one can take that meeting from us."

Luka

We toast Luka
with his favorite cognac.
The river is ready.

The river breathes cold.
Our words to Luka
are a kind of lullaby.

Luka, Luka, Luka,
with your plastic arm.
You're drifting far away.

Luka, Luka, Luka,
your daughter
will get your medal.

Lullaby

I go to bed and turn
to face the wall.
Please send mum and dad
and grandma back.

I'll go to bed, little fish
will drift to sleep in Dnister.
Let my sister and me
fall soon to sleep.

Little fish goes to sleep
in the muddy water.
Don't let those people
come to our house again.

Little fish dreams of warm currents
and the stream.
Just like me, little fish
visits her loved ones in a dream.

Please send our mum
and dad and grandma back
to my sister Irusya and me
in a dream.

II.
Voices

Mum

You'll become
a man of rock.
A hard and strong and slightly
cracked man.

Like I've always said,
not a stumbling block,
not a cornerstone.
But a stone impervious
to water.

Now we both know:
there's no such thing as leave
from war, only parting.
But may each one of us
who taught you softness,
also add hardness
to your body of stone.

This isn't a farewell,
but I tell you: I'm always on your shoulder.
You, the Softest Child on Earth,
from now on you're a stone.
Amen.

Grandma

Don't tell me where you are. But tell me,
where you are,
did they grind the wheat already?
I've heard on the news that in Donbas
they won't bring the harvest in.
But your grandpa doesn't believe it
and neither do I.

1st September was the same old, same old.
The kids went off to school,
our little girl to kindergarten.
At first, I cried and didn't want to see
the back-to-school festivities.
But your grandad went
so I did, too.

It's because I keep crying, you know.
The little ones wore suits.
Our little girl wore ribbons in her hair.
But this September,
some no longer own a suit.
Some no longer have any tears to cry.
And some
no longer have grandchildren.

Lord, oh Lord.

Don't tell me, don't tell me where you are.
But where you are now,
has the rain come already?
It was raining here yesterday,
but not much.
Such a gentle rain,
so gentle
you could take a child by the hand
and walk together
down the road.

***

"Please look after yourself, take care."
(A candle burns in the kitchen like an oracle.)
Please let him take care out there, and someday
he can tell us all about it, if he wants to.

He changed schools and his name,
sat alone in the yard all the time,
dropped out of university twice,
ran away from home, wandering in the woods
until morning. But now
please let him take care.

I took care of him so well when he was little.
In fact, we all took care of him.
Now blood burns in his veins, his forehead sweats
as if he'd quarrelled with his stepdad again.

"Please remember to take care of yourself out there."
(The candle waxes strong, the flame still burns).
He embraced her warmly and clumsily.
Outside it was thundering.

Fedir

Lyuba, – he said to his daughter.
I had this trident pin in Siberia.
Always carried it with me
and with me it came back.

Lyuba, when I die,
pin this trident on me.
I always carried it with me
and I want to lie down with it.

Love, Lyuba, be a love and don't cry.
When they come to close the coffin,
take this trident off me.

It's not right for it
to rot in the ground.

Trident (colloquially known as the *'tryzub'*) is a symbol featured in the national
coat of arms of Ukraine; it is often worn in miniature as a pin or pendant.

Rosary

When he left, he took my rosary.
When he left, I knew he'd come back.
July 2015, it was a hot day.
He said: I'm going so far away,
I want to take the thought of you with me.
July 2015, and my poor dad
walking round, making such a fuss, hiding his face.
Dad was trying to be strong, he only cried once,
when the backpack and everything were gone.
Your uncle had already gone, and the road was so tough
so many of them went, and they went through so much,
they churned up so much dirt with their feet
that a garden grew behind their backs by spring.
Not all of them found the path back home.

You both have the same hands, hair, and home.
How many years have passed since then, seven?
My dad, your grandad, is trying to hide.
I'm not hiding, I know that those footprints
haven't yet healed, haven't been bandaged by grass.
Your uncle can't walk with you,
but now you've got his strange footsteps to follow.
You've got his hands and his hair. So go.
Your grandad is in hiding. When you come,
go find him and laugh. He'll smile
right back at you from behind the gate.
So many of you are going, so may you always
have the things that my brother had:
a cross, a string, these worn-out beads.

Partisan Street

1

Ah, Kiryukha, he's our regiment's adopted child,
the only one left in the entire street.
He wasn't here when the Russians came,
his grandad got him out in the nick of time.
There's not a scratch on him.
Main thing is, there's not a scratch on him.

In our town, there are plenty of kids,
and we've got a playground,
we made it ourselves,
swings, roundabouts, the lot.

I even told 'em,
with all my nerve, I told 'em:
Just don't touch this one thing,
don't touch our playground.

And as I recall,
we're all standing there
and they're driving their tank.
And one of them sticks his head
out of it, laughing,
and drives right over our playground.

2

One night, he came by,
a Buryat, such a scumbag.
And I was so full of rage,
so full of Ukrainian woman rage,
that I saw him off with a slipper.
Him with his machine gun, me with my slipper.

And then I kicked him in the butt
for good measure.
Later, the fear hit me, I got scared.
But in that moment I was so full of rage,
proper woman rage.

You know, boys, it's the first time
in eight months
I've eaten so nicely with a fork.
I feel like Snow White.

3

Many things happened,
but we lived on hope.
We'd waited so long.

Why do they keep pushing in?
Why do they do it?

Don't they understand,
they won't get their way?
We won't let 'em.

Many of us on the street stayed.
Some left but
many stayed.
We live on Partisan Street, don't you know.
We, dear boys, live on hope.

Valya

He and Valya really liked each other.
They'd gather things from her garden
and cook together.
Valya even flirted with him a little,
but only in a neighbourly way.

I don't know how it happened.
A series of misunderstandings
and by morning we assumed
she already knew.

But then Valya was fetching onions,
and washing them, and asking:
"So how's our boy?
Has he made it to the hospital yet?"

Kiryukha

You won't say: we were here.
Pressing against each other
in dugouts won back from the Russians.
And only later, snow came.

We were here. But we'll
never be asked about it.
Only Kiryukha,
our regiment's adopted child (like she said)
– the only one left in the entire street –
will someday remember
the crushed Snickers bars and the freezing
cold of that terrible wartime December.

Brace yourself, they'll ask you about other things,
so brace yourself:
Where's your leg?
Where are your laughing friends?
Where's your youth?
You, an old man of twenty,
 still dreaming of death and crushed Snickers bars?

They won't ask the most important thing:
where were you
when Santa
in that terrible wartime December
left a plastic supermarket bag
by Kiryukha's bed,
a bag with our crushed Snickers bars
and tangerines.
The ones with seeds,
but oh so sweet.

The Little Guy

He took my machine gun away from me
at once. I came clean:
I wanted to use it on myself.
And he took my machine gun away at once.

Did I let them all down?
Everyone says I let them down so badly.
But I had to come clean, don't you understand?

Do you know why I didn't do it?
I almost pulled the trigger,
but then I started crying and had to come clean.
You know why?

I thought of the little guy.
He made this bracelet for me.
I thought about my wife
and the little guy.
And he's not even my son!
Not even mine,
do you get it?

Misha

You say: I pissed myself, I can't make it.
But we all get scared.

I recall how you told us once
about your Mum and your farm.
And about your special someone,
the one you keep running into
no matter how far you both go.
Isn't that a Motherland?

Think about the farm and that special girl.
About the sun, for goodness' sake.
Today the sun looks like
it's laughing at us,
as if it's that boy
from the sapper platoon –
the one with red hair, remember?
He couldn't even pronounce the letter "r".

***

When we take off our bulletproof vests,
helmets, coats, jackets and gloves,
and sit down to eat tangerines by the stove,
we are children again,
and sometimes I think
you're in the next room.

In the village
a local woman
called out to her child: "My son!".

And every one of us
turned around.

***

Literature won't kill anybody,
a poem won't shield you from a bullet,
books won't save us from mortars,
writing won't find the missing,
so there's not much point to it now.

But we had draughts and heat here,
and the stench of corpses from the ravine
was reaching the dugout.
We tried using an air freshener,
but on the third day it ran out.

So I read
the selected poems of Stus
and smelt the book
after every poem.

Vasyl Stus (1938–1985) is widely regarded as one of Ukraine's foremost poets.
He was an active member of the Ukrainian dissident movement. Because of his
political convictions, his works were banned by the Soviet regime and he spent
13 years in detention until his death in a Soviet forced labour camp for political
prisoners on September 4, 1985.

***

Boots, armour, and Kevlar helmets.
Who are we?
We're kids.

May this land enter our breast
and may it
hurt.

May this land bleed like a wound.
Unknown.
Familiar.

May our machine guns never jam.
Where are we?
We're home.

Evac

Faster, bandage him, faster.
No matter how tired you are.
What good does this poem
do for the dead?

Tighten it just above the knees,
call the doc.
Do something for him before he
crosses over to the other side.

A medic comes running from the trench
through the smoke.
His temples throb
with a call sign.

Now you can close his eyes.
It's July.
You can hear the men
sobbing.

Breathe out, then take
a deep breath in.
Copy, we have a still one.
Copy.

An 'evac' is Ukrainian military slang for a vehicle with which medical personnel
evacuate the injured.

Stus

The shells are flying,
what a grand time.
And fury, fury, fury.
And those who died are rising
to stand with us.
Smiling and stubborn,
ripped out of the earth
to laugh in the face of death,
despising it,
the way in times
like these
only the dead can.
Those inured to temptation
and steeled for loss.
– Next, name?
– V. Stus.
– Rank?
– Soldier.
The fire of blazing fury
never went out in your face.
Your dead are with you;
they're on your side.
No one turns a blind eye,
no-one's above the fray.
Just fury, fury, fury.

No living man
will be scared
no dead man
killed.

L. K.

You've become so terribly grown up.
I've always been more mature.
Now it's the other way round.

What can I say?
Nobody asked if I was ready,
if you had my permission to go
or if something would creep out
of my lungs at night,
stopping in my throat,
making my chest cold,
squeezing my stomach.

Do you remember that time
you caught a mouse in my dorm?
Maybe it's the same mouse
scratching in your trench.
I know it sounds silly
but I freeze with you
when I think of those trenches.

My terribly grown-up friend,
don't ask me about home.
The last time I felt at home
was when I met you from work
that summer.
We were riding an electric scooter
and buses were passing by.
And you were holding down my dress
as it billowed in the wind.

***

And then I took off my T-shirt and we stood
naked
up to our waists,
ready
for anything.
Pressing our chests against each other.

Who are you to me?
You are a slow-moving star.
Who am I to you?
I am that feeling
when you stand in front of a poem
like an open window
and step forward.

So I took my T-shirt off,
and we pressed our chests against each other.
And you said: every evening I wonder
what it's like to be your heart.

Who are you to me?
You are the one who is always chest-to-chest.
Who am I to you?
I am the one who is chest-to-chest.

Slow Star at the Open Window,
I couldn't tell you my heart's truth,
because how do you dare tell someone
something only they know?

***

How long have we been talking like this?
You said when you dreamt of me last time
I looked like a shoal of sad fish.
And today, I found scales
in my bed.

Again: how long have we been talking like this?
You said you bought a blue envelope
and kept placing poems inside it.
Could you do me a favour?
Wet its edges with your
saliva.
Bend them with your
fingers.
Press them with your
hands.
And, for the last time:
how long have we been talking like this?

The shoal of sad fish swims,
 but never gets very far.
They keep
 bumping into your fingers.
They keep
 curling into your hands.
They keep falling asleep
 in your saliva.

***

"..., but why do you call me that?"
she will ask.
"Why do you call me a city?

You always write about the city
when I know it's about me.
You write about buses,
and my hand starts itching.
You write about railway stations,
and I wake in the middle of the night
and can't get back to sleep.
You write about cobblestones
and I feel
a lump in my throat
that I can't cough up.

I want to understand
why you call me a city."

And I won't say a word, thinking:

When she frowns,
barely perceptible
tram tracks
appear above her brows.

It would be so nice not to get off
at the last stop.

***

For the first time, the distance between us
is measured by army checkpoints.
I've already moved. In the village
I saw my first drone, flying like a hornet.

When I was little I wasn't the jittery sort.
Even now I'm not afraid of fire.
But this move feels like a dislocated bone
that won't click back into place by itself.

So I'm humming your name
like a song, like a lullaby; I climb into it
like those geese into the branches,
like it's the first word I ever learned.

***

It was winter and
we made it through.
Heavy march
and first losses.
Take his unimaginable
soldier's sorrow;
it's yours now
to have and to hold.

His soldier's delight,
blast concussions, exhaustion,
his raspy breath after battles,
and all he has endured;
you lug it home
after him.

A battered gate, a bench,
that's all.
A limping man
has reached the front door.
She follows him,
carrying his backpack,
his water,
and the weight
of his everything else.

***

You walk through wetlands to the river. To breathe,
to read his letters and search for the poems in them,
to tend to this shrapnel wound which you call
love, though it's something bigger.
So good to have this river and its bank.
And you call him darling.
It all moves so fast and there's never enough,
so let this moment last a little longer,
this feeling between the ribs and in the spine:
"He forgets everything but me".

Look, here's the river and the wetlands,
this country drenched and sticky under your skin,
this country that you sense by touch
as it spills out of you – but until then
you can never really understand it.
It's good that it's April soon.
It's good to have his poems and letters.
He forgets everything, but you
will neither fade nor pass.
Something between the ribs,
under the skin,
in the spine.

***

If I don't make it, or fail
– September's far off, expect winds –
take this strange hope in my place;
 sleep with it, talk to it when you miss me.
Let it believe what I couldn't believe,
 let it stay silent, laugh, or lie face up,
 let it absorb the scent from your T-shirts and skin,
keep it close, in your room.
If I don't make it, if I can't go on,
 hold on to this strange hope as you look over the edge.
September's far off: expect sorrow;
September's far off: wait for me.

***

Here you are, so cautious,
on the riverbank, its slippery silt.
How much time has passed
since all of this began?

This sticky river carried away
boys from my platoon.
I remember you were
by my side from the start.

Here you are, so furious, so tender,
your sensitive, weather-bitten lips.
We stand in the silt
while others are carried by the river.

Perhaps someone will ask
about all that you endured
shoulder to shoulder with me,
bringing on burning memories.

Maybe you'll tell someone
about the river's sticky bank and bed.
"Don't yield," you say to me,
and that is why I won't yield.

I remember you said it
before anyone else.
That's how I could get to this point
and not yield.

***

The lights will never go out
in your house. Look;
it won't be the same as before,
but it won't be deserted.

Don't worry about the walls, don't cry.
Light will blaze from the ceiling to the floor.
All the electric cables in the national grid
will be wired to power your house alone.

Electricians working up high on the pylons
won't doze off on their shifts.
When I stop and think about it,
everything's worked out just fine.

This spring will become a memory. Tonight
the lines of your body and face are vague,
just like the high-voltage lines
through the hoar-frosted window.

These days will linger on.
These names, once spoken, never fade.
We'll see each other at the end
close to the other side.

Someone will drive past your window
at high speed, making lots of noise.
When I die, I'll become the electricity
that lights up your house,

your wrinkled T-shirts and jeans,
and your street after rain.
I'll be the light in your bathroom.
A desk lamp. A lantern.

***

May you always have the words
to write about tram stops wet with rain,
and the weary light of the local laundrette
and the pigeons puffed up underneath it.

And those lying somewhere, young and hungry –
their naked bodies aroused and quivering.
The babies sleeping in their cradles,
the dead sleeping in the Field of Mars.

May you always have a dictionary nearby.
Write about the first person you loved, who is gone,
or the heart, fragile and fiery,
or even about me.

About dirty puddles on the street
or a tram scaring up the flock of birds.
You know, I often wonder
how you choose the best words.

But today you've lost them,
and all of your phrases
jam in your throat like clothes
in a broken washing machine.

Find them, cough them out and collect them,
drum them out on your keyboard.
In the street, people are tired and downhearted;
a tram is passing through a stop wet with rain.

***

Say hello to the children.
Tell them a bird in my chest
has driven me East again.
Tell them not to be scared.

I know you don't like the bird,
but it's not as though I chose her over you.
It's just that she wakes up,
stretches
and has such wings –
how can I not go?

Send love to the children,
just as they send drawings
to me and the boys.
Like the one
where nine little fingers were traced
but the marker ran out
on the tenth.
And the one that I've been carrying
in my coat pocket since summer.
And especially the one
of a wooden bird feeder.

That one's my favourite.

***

And the city says:

My petrol stations, my bus terminals.
When she sees him
it's like a dog running to its owner.
Even though the kennel's far off. Even though it's raining.

Forehead, stomach, right then left shoulder.
Perhaps it's easier to live this way.
But how can these two build me
with their hands bound?

My petrol stations, my bus terminals.
When he sees her
it's like something is growing out of his throat.
It's hard to breathe
until you set it free.

Forehead, stomach, right then left shoulder.
Probably, poems
are things that one person needed to tell another
but couldn't.

Children

When we speak of hope
we're actually speaking
of children.

I'm grateful for the memory of you
which still passes through me
though it was all so long ago.
And someday all children
will squint at the sun.
And those of us who survived
will see
that none of this was in vain.

Here we rarely speak of hope
or patriotism
or the Motherland.
But when we speak
it is always about children.
And when I remember you,
I imagine the child you were,
squinting at the sun.

Those of us who survive
will be silent for a long time.
Because who needs words
about hope
when it's standing right in front of you?
Wearing muddy shorts,
scratching the mosquito bites on its arms,
flashing its milk teeth
at the sun.

Prayer

With the swimmers, swim,
with the travelers, travel,
as they say in church.

With the one who was raped
and is expecting a child,
breathe, breathe, breathe.
With the child whose hair has gone grey,
prepare a backpack for school.

With the frostbitten, freeze,
with the shellshocked, vomit in the trench.
With the tank commander,
who's been missing since October,
be found, be pieced together
from scattered body parts.
Consecrated particles
as they say in church.

And also be
with the one who eats pot noodles with cold water;
with the one who was captured but will never talk;
with the one who was conceived
but didn't get born.
And be with the one
who didn't get to give birth.

And also be
with the two girls
somewhere in the Rivne region, do you remember?
We were driving to the east, in a convoy,
and they stood watching at the roadside,
and put their hands on their hearts.

And then I understood everything.

***

We quarrelled again
about when to celebrate your birth.
But, you know,
Bethlehem was bombed
on both 25th December and January 7th.

No manger, no sheep, no
maternity ward, no
kindergarten, no
playground.

When you get a bit older and start talking,
tell your mum to tell my mum
how she should bear
all of this.

Trisagion

Holy Mighty –
Holy Fortified –
Holy Assigned-to-our-House.

Yesterday those asleep in the womb
were woken up.
A bonus to our citizenship:
gaining combat experience
before your date of birth.

The woman says: I will bite
through the throats of strangers.
They say to the woman: bite
through your own umbilical cord.

Holy Shelled –
Holy Sharpshooter –
Holy Shattered – deliver
the child.

The Trisagion is a standard hymn of the Divine Liturgy in most of the Eastern
Orthodox, Western Orthodox, Oriental Orthodox, and Eastern Catholic churches.

The Izyum Communion

***

These are our bodies
broken for us.
But no forgiveness of sin.

These are our bodies
that break apart so easily
when exhumed from the earth.

These are our forests, and these are our crosses.
And these are the bodies
broken only for us.

Now you see clearly:
we're so much like your son.
But no forgiveness of sin.
Look:
the same bones stick out,
the same blood and water.
But no forgiveness of sin.
Listen:
the same scream, the same silence.

This is what the Izyum Communion
looks like.
These are our forests and these are our crosses,
and the living dig up the dead, saying:
these are our bodies, these are our bodies.
We look so much like your son.
These are our bodies, look at our bodies.
We've been like your son for so long.
So many bodies, look, so many bodies.
We're the younger son
who will never forgive.

Izyum is a city in Kharkiv region, Ukraine, nearly destroyed during Russian occupation in 2022. After the liberation of the city by the Ukrainian forces in September 2022, a mass burial site of over 450, mostly civilians, was found with signs of torture and mutilation on bodies.

The Divine Liturgy is the Holy Mass in Eastern Christianity.

Nastya

Before great-grandma Nastya died
in 2007, there were already six of us;

only boys are being born,
– she said – looks like there'll be a war.

She knew what war was.
She knew how it was during Holodomor.
She knew how to raise children on her own.
In her final year, she knew
how to whack apples with her cane
to make them soft to eat and to make the little ones laugh.

But she didn't know that two granddaughters
already had new life growing in their bellies.
And a baby would be born in July –
a little girl.

Holodomor was a famine inflicted on Ukraine in the early twentieth century by the
Stalin-led Soviet regime, which resulted in the death of 4 million Ukrainians. It is
widely recognized internationally as an act of genocide against the Ukrainian people.

III.
The Beginning,
The End,
The Beginning

The 1st Letter
to the Corinthians

Love is patient, love is kind.
It does not envy, it does not boast;
love fears with a primal fear,
but walks on;
love could have surrendered, abandoned everything,
but it walks on.
And sometimes love gets shot in the legs,
or shell fragments get stuck in them,
or its legs get blown off.
Then love is carried by its friends.

Love digs trenches and lives in them,
gnawing on ice from a hacked-up plastic bottle,
when it suffers thirst at minus twenty.
Love goes out on combat duty,
enters firing positions
with hernias, fever, prostatitis,
with blast concussions, asthma and allergies,
with a high probability
of not making it back,
thinking all the while about
the one most important to them.
Love bears all things, believes all things,
hopes all things, endures all things!

Love distinguishes the sounds
of a Grad rocket launching, mines exploding and tanks
advancing.
Love's eyes ache
when it stares through a thermal imager too long.
Love wakes up at night
when mice in the dugout
crawl under its coat.
Sometimes love
vomits at length in the woodland after a heavy fight.
And sometimes love closes its friends' eyes,
wraps them in sleeping bags
and carries them away.

Love never fails.
But where there are prophecies, they will cease;
where there are tongues, they will be stilled;
where there is knowledge, it will pass away.
Because sometimes when the shelling ceases,
friends close love's eyes,
wrap it in sleeping bags
and carry it away.

And then it passes on
to the living.

Why do we need poetry?

For a long time I had no answer to this question. I told myself that I didn't know.

After the full-scale invasion began, I stopped writing. Since the age of seventeen, I had believed that literature was my purpose in life, I thought that being a writer was something that carried weight and had meaning. And suddenly it turned out that there was no meaning at all. What can you write when children are being pulled from under the rubble? In what order do you arrange words to ease the pain? I decided that writing was pointless.

But I was wrong. Time needed to pass because it is impossible to write about today in the old language. It had to be reinvented. I had to lose faith in writing, admit that literature was helpless, begin hating all writers, forget every poem. I had to give up on language completely. And start from the beginning.

Let's go back to the beginning. Now I have the answer. Why do we need poetry in a time of war? Why do we keep writing these poems, reading them, sharing them with each other like communion wafers or cigarettes? Why do we sometimes need to read something to feel love or even hate more fiercely? Why do we need poems?

To feel less lonely.

Of course, poetry does more than just this. It's also a way of approaching another person's experience, the chance to read what you yourself don't dare articulate, it's a path to you and other people. It is many things, but the core of the need for poetry in these terrible times lies in it making us feel less lonely. Words have meaning when they are necessary, the only possible words. We must speak those words to one another, share them like communion wafers or cigarettes. It is true that they can't protect anyone, can't bring anyone back. They can't ease the pain. But they can remind us that we're not facing this alone. There is a lot of pain but there are also a lot of us. And this is our shared pain.

Therefore, if there is something worth writing about during the war, it's not the war itself, but the people. Because the significant thing isn't that the war has happened to us, but that it is us that the war happened to. When Russians attacked, we chose to fight back, we are resisting. We fight and we overcome our fear. We bury our dead and we cry. We love and we embrace. The very embodiment of horror has come here, but we were here. It is us who were here. And we are not going anywhere.

2

Sometimes letters from children make it to the frontline. During the toughest times we'd read and pass them around, sharing them like we did with communion wafers or cigarettes. Or poems. We'd read them and not one of us would feel lonely.

I keep several dozen in one of my rucksacks and some in my pocket Bible. I know many of them by heart. Just like in poems, the words in these letters are the only possible ones. Even if some are riddled with spelling mistakes or you can hardly read them because the pen started leaking halfway through. And these letters, notes and drawings, the pure embodiment of pain and hope, have a great impact on soldiers. Perhaps we wouldn't be able to make it through the toughest times without them. And, most certainly, it is their letters that make it possible for me to speak as I do through this book.

And because the words of children do so much for me, it is only right that my words should do something for them. Together with Old Lion Publishing, we decided to donate all profits made from the sales of this book in Ukrainian to The Voices of Children Charity Foundation to help children who have suffered from the war. If you wish to make your own contribution, you may do so via *https://voices.org.ua/en/donat/* or the QR code below.

Literature itself can't protect or save anyone, it's true. But we can.

And we are still here.

Artur

MORE ON JANTAR

Jantar is an independent publisher based in London that has been praised widely for its choice of texts, artwork, editorial rigour and use of very rare and sometimes unique fonts in all its books. Jantar's guiding principle is to select, publish and make accessible previously inaccessible works of European Literary Fiction through translations into English … texts 'trapped in amber'.

Since its foundation in 2011, Jantar's list consisted, mostly, of works of Literary Fiction. In 2023, we began to broaden our mission to include works of Science Fiction. In 2024, we have expanded our list even further by launching The Amber Poets series with *We Were Here*.

Being Jantar, we began our new SF list with the first recognised works in the genre written in Czech and Slovak. *Newton's Brain* by Jakub Arbes and published in a new translation by David Short, was first published in 1877, 18 years before The Time Machine by H.G. Wells. Arbes was much admired by Emile Zola. Our second SF title was written in an uncodified version of 'Old Slovak' in 1856. *The Science of the Stars* by Gustav Reuss is arguably the first title to feature a balloon travelling to the moon. It is certainly the first to appear in any version of Slovak.

In March 2024, we published our fourth title by Balla, *Among the Ruins*, a gentle satire featuring a fragile middle-aged woman who still believes she is living in the 1980s and spends a lot of her time writing to her therapist, a hopeless drunk who cannot even look after himself. It is never clear whether either characters have met. In July, we published *Winterberg's Last Journey* by Jaroslav Rudiš. A journey through Central European history described by The Spectator as 'a beautiful tragicomedy'.

Much more Literary Fiction, Science Fiction and Poetry will be published next year. Highlights include the much-anticipated new translation of *The Grandmother* by Božena Němcová, one of the three founding works of modern Czech Literature. This new and complete translation will show, for the first time to English-language readers, the subversive, feminist, anti-theological and anti-Habsburg elements in this classic text.

These titles and all our other titles can be purchased
postage-free world-wide from our website:
www.JantarPublishing.com